We Love Lucy

Our Little Lion Dog

Copyright, Credits and Disclaimers

Cover design and interior photography by Carrie Taylor Goldberg, except: “First Morning Greeting”, “Ever Deepening Bonds”, “Wading into the Gulf”, “In Mama’s Arms” and author profile pictures taken by William S. Goldberg. Used with permission.

Many people along the path have met Lucy, either live or online. She has a big extended family of honorary aunts and uncles, grandmas and grandpas. You know who you are, even if you have not been mentioned by name. We appreciate all the tenderness you have shown toward our little dog.

ISBN # (paperback) 979-8-218-90800-3

Endorsements

Read what other "Dog Moms" have observed about this author's heart for their dogs as well as our Lucy.

~ ~ ~

Ember Rose was a beautiful American Mastiff. She loved when people would visit our home. I remember Ember warming up to Carrie right away. Ember was huge and Carrie was easily moved by our pup. She could knock her over coming in for a snuggle. The time Ember tried to go through the cat door to greet Carrie was also quite comical. Picture a big Mastiff head sticking out of the frame! She was so friendly.

Lucy is one lucky dog. She has the most loving human parents any dog could ask for. Lucy is loved and cared for so well. I'd almost call her a pampered pooch. She is such a sweet dog. Her needs are met and then some. Lucy loves the attention. Carrie is so attentive with her fur baby. All dogs should be as lucky.

~ *Shelley*

Pippin was my first furry child while I was in university. Carrie, my housemate, treated him as one of the family. She would always take the time to greet him as she came in and would often sit with him to read on the sofa.

Lucy is definitely Carrie's furry child. The nest she makes for Lucy in the back seat on road trips is amazing! Every comfort is considered: window views, snacks, water, passageway to the front...it is all there.

~ *Angie*

Riding in Comfort

Tributes

Below are my key memories of three little female dogs to whom I became particularly attached – long before I met Lucy. Their dog moms and I miss them.

~ ~ ~

Cheryl's Beagle Abby:

Abby's eyes would light up as I approached the window of her house. We'd often hang out together while my friend Cheryl was at work or out of town.

After I moved across the country, I returned to visit a couple of years later. As soon as Abby saw me, she danced with delight all over me.

Lucy lounges on Abby's beige rug.

Sylvia's Poodle Ella:

Ella would excitedly bark at the door when I arrived at my aunt's place on the farm. Then she'd twirl around, squealing with excitement over the attention I gave her.

One morning, I awoke to Ella jumping on the bed, poking the covers aside and licking my eyes open! Some evenings as I relaxed in an armchair, she cradled in my arms.

Lucy walks with Ella's pink harness.

Sharon's Shih Tzu Molly:

Molly would comfort me through the loss of my grandmother, then my father nine months later. She'd rest beside me as I prepared for their memorials.

When I came to visit, my friend Sharon had some new trick for Molly to show me. This spunky dog suddenly took a refreshing plunge in a park water fountain during our last walk together.

Lucy rests on Molly's pink blanket.

Preface

As I sit down to begin this book about our precious little gift from God, Lucy positions herself under the desk by my feet. The ambience is set for this writer.

Who is Lucy? Her ancestral origins are Tibet. She's a royal canine. Shih Tzu dogs, Mandarin meaning 'little lion', used to dwell in palaces. Once treasured in China, during the communist revolution they became almost extinct. Thankfully, a British woman and an officer provided safe passage for a few to England. Some U.S. soldiers after WWII became endeared to this new breed and introduced them to North America. Our Lucy was born at Roy Lake, South Dakota, July 10th, 2011.

Return to her Birthplace

Loyal Royal Canine

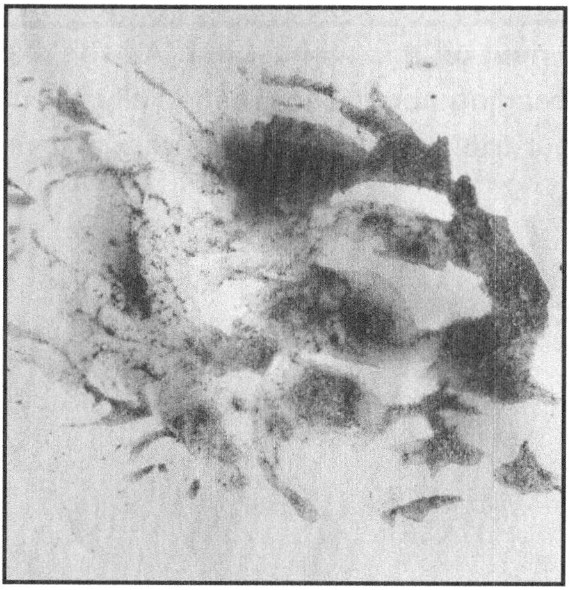

Lucy's Paw Print Signature

Acknowledgments

Foremost, I thank God for bringing this precious creature into our lives. Secondly, I thank my husband William for choosing her from among the puppies offered by a kind neighbor named Joan. Our family and friends have readily embraced our adorable Lucy.

Earlier this year William and I had serious concerns for Lucy's health. I already had in mind to write a book about our little dog, but the cost of saving Lucy's life took me on a different publication route.

Guided by God's wisdom, covered by much prayer and following our new veterinary team's treatment plan, Lucy continues to enjoy life with us.

Special thanks to Colonel Cathy for her eager editorial input on this manuscript. As she expressed, "I loved reading about Lucy, especially after meeting her on your trip! ... Your book is a work of love!"

Under Daddy's Protective Hand

Fluffy Little Puppy

Contents

Mutual Adoption

Married life began with a dog. Lucy came with the husband. William's house became her home, then eventually mine too. We are family.

Let's back up a bit first. After mutual friend Hannah introduced my future husband to me, we began to correspond via email. Next, I received a text that he wanted to come to Canada to meet me. As the *Proverbs* say (11:14), there's safety in seeking counsel from others, so I selected a few trusted friends and family members to meet William.

During a special supper hosted by Aunt Sylvia, I looked around for her dog Ella, who usually showed her utter delight whenever I arrived to visit. My aunt motioned toward William; there was Ella seated on his lap! Thus, her dog became a sign to my aunt, who stated emphatically, "The dogs like him; he's in!"

Shortly after William began his long road trip back south, I received a text from Uncle Bob, "What are you going to do with him?" Like a puppy, I chose to keep him. William passed the doggy detector test.

Years before we met, William was out walking around the neighborhood one day when someone asked him if he wanted to pick out a puppy. From a nearby neighbor, William adopted Lucy at about six months of age. She was the smallest and the most playful of her siblings. If only I could have seen her then!

It was not until Lucy was five years old that I first met her in her new home. William had already visited me in the fall, and our relationship was progressing. By spring, I came to see his natural habitat. The city reminded me of where I grew up, just outside of Toronto, Canada. Initially, Lucy showed curiosity over this strange woman wandering around the kitchen. She followed at my heels, sniffing, apparently trying to ascertain whether I was trustworthy. My first morning, waking in the guest room, Lucy greeted me with a lick on my face. That doggy kiss endeared her to me.

William and I became engaged that spring and married by the following fall. During our first year anniversary month, I began earnestly nesting in my new abode. That's when the process of mutual adoption took place; I adopted Lucy and she, me. Our bonds grew closer as we worked through her jealousy over William. Eventually Lucy accepted my status as the alpha female.

Daddy's little girl became also Mama's baby girl.

First Morning Greeting

Ever Deepening Bonds

Five in One

Lucy was William's pick of the puppies. Her adoptive home no longer stands but the route nearest it remains our favorite one to walk. Periodically William is in touch with the kind lady who offered Lucy to him. Recently Joan returned to the area to visit and saw how well Lucy is cared for. She is the only one remaining among her canine siblings and parents.

Referring to her three-striped colors, a clerk in a souvenir shop called her a "Neapolitan" dog. Lucy has a silvery gray head, a creamy white band around her shoulders, and a back full of golden tan curls.

Accenting her soft and shiny coat is her pom pom tail, curled around, riding high. Like her floppy pigtail ears, it contains highlights of black and auburn. Her tender tootsies and underbelly are white.

The first noticeable features are Lucy's big brown bright eyes. Her eyebrows are quite expressive. She has a cute button nose and dainty mouth which at times appears to smile. Being a Shih Tzu, her snout is shorter than most dogs.

Lucy is our only pet, yet she has qualities of five animals in one. Although she's mostly quiet, she certainly barks like a dog, with tones that are pleasing to our ears. When she licks her front paws and rubs them to clean her face, she reminds me of a cat. As she circles around, fluffing up her bed before settling into it, she's akin to a bird making her nest. Eager to return home, with her rabbit design rear legs, she hops up the steps. She often snorts similar to a pig, which means she's satisfied.

During a 2024 road trip, on a morning walk before resuming our travels through Iowa, we met a woman who called out to us from her balcony. I looked up to see it filled with plants, along with a sign marked: "Porch Therapy". The local resident remarked exuberantly, "That there's a show dog; look how she carries herself!" Yes, that's our humble little Lucy.

Gold, Crème, and Silver Top

Big Brown Bright Eyes

Right at this moment, I'm looking at them – those big brown bright eyes. Lucy is relaxing in the cool green grass across from me as I write. Somewhere I read that dogs can hug you with their eyes. For humans, eyes are believed to be a window into the soul. So I think that when Lucy gazes into my eyes that she's embracing my soul.

Given the rounded shape of her face, resembling an Asian lion, her eyes especially stand out when she's excited. They actually bulge out and show some white when she anticipates something tasty. What pleasure there is in watching her gently accept a morsel from my outstretched hand. Rather than simply gulping it down, she takes a moment to acknowledge me with her eyes.

Back in 2019, I recall all too vividly another look in Lucy's eyes: fear. It was late at night and I'd fallen asleep on the couch while watching a long movie. Lucy woke me, nervously drawing my attention out the window. Trees in our front yard were swaying almost horizontally! I grabbed my phone and noticed an alert to seek shelter immediately. But we have no basement. While I quickly considered where to take refuge, suddenly we heard a rumbling sound and looked into each other's eyes.

Next, what sounded like an explosion came from our front entrance, followed by what appeared to be smoke but without any scent. Cautiously I peered out and found a large tree bough protruding from the entryway ceiling, blocking our exit. Rapidly I emptied the biggest plastic bin we had, placing it underneath the gaping hole to catch incoming rain. Insulation from the attic was strewn around, helping to absorb moisture.

Collecting a few essential items, I scooped up Lucy and exited through the back, over a fence, and sought refuge from the storm with our neighbors whose lights were still on. Readily they welcomed us, wrapped Lucy in a towel and held her calmly. I called my husband at work to brief him on our housing situation. Afterward I contacted the insurance company. Our neighbors invited us to stay with them until emergency repairs were completed on our roof, electrical inspections were done, and debris was cleaned up. Lucy and I survived our first tornado trauma together!

A far more welcome memory of Lucy looking out the window is upon arriving home from work. Daily, those big brown bright eyes are there, eagerly awaiting each of us to return. The closer we approach, Lucy's eyes light up even brighter.

Oh So Adorable

Hopeful Yet Content

Attentive Auburn Ears

Those floppy ears, sometimes dipping in her water dish or dragging in her food bowl, perk up to show Lucy is attentive to what we're saying. She may not understand everything, but she certainly seems to put forth a great effort. There's no question she is listening intently.

Smart dog that she is, she grasps the tone of a question and attempts some sort of response. Sometimes it's a little shift, or jumping motion while lying down, head raised. Or, she may wag her tail. She anticipates something good is about to happen.

Her auburn ears give her a stylish, feminine look. She loves to receive a massage behind her ears, tilting her head toward the trusted hand. She doesn't mind a gentle brushing, so long as I don't move the grooming tool down to her cheeks.

Lucy readily recognizes my whistle, although not always discerning from what direction. If one of us is away for awhile, we let Lucy hear our spouse's voice over the phone. In fact, several of our long-distance friends greet Lucy over the phone or in video chats.

Like other dogs, she enjoys a good squeaky toy. Her rubber fish outlasts them all. She throws and fetches it herself, although sometimes she lets us play too! Lucy's lamb still squeaks on one foot and from the belly area, where her tiny sharp teeth have not yet punctured.

Certain sounds we try to shield Lucy from are thunder and fireworks. Before either source of loud bangs are imminent, we try to let Lucy do her business out in the yard. Once indoors, the outer noises are masked by fans or air conditioners. She finds comfort staying close by our side.

Like her mama, Lucy's not partial to loud music or TV programs. But she seems to like being sung to. I've come up with spontaneous custom songs about her. Occasionally she's entertained with an accompanying dance. Last July, while out on a walk, some neighborhood kids sang "Happy Birthday" to Lucy. How sweet.

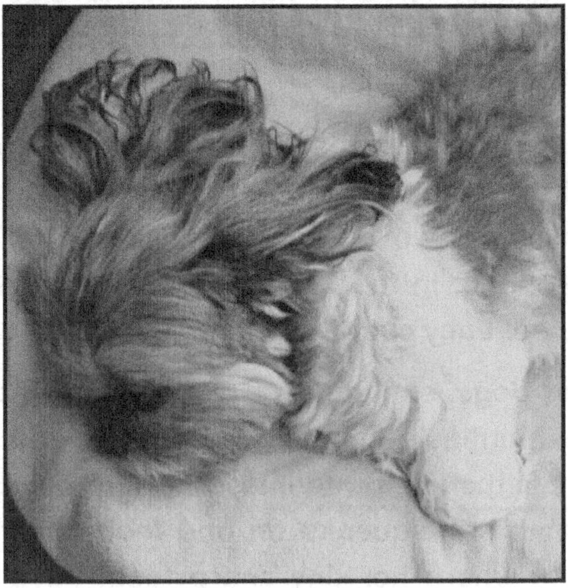

She's All Ears

Give Mama a Kiss

Before I'd earned the right to be her mama, Lucy gave me my first kiss – as a visiting guest. That was the beginning of our bond.

Her soft pink tongue giving a lick on my nose is her way of saying thank you. She appreciates help with cleaning her eyes and trimming excess fur out of her line of vision. Occasionally a chewy piece of bone or treat gets stuck inside of her cheek, much like a caramel might with us. The first time I noticed her mouth in an "O" shape, opening and closing like a fish, I wondered what was going on. It was a comical sight. Swabbing my finger inside, I discovered the hidden morsel and loosed it, letting Lucy finish chewing it. With a quick slurp of her tongue, she expressed thanks for retrieving her tasty treasure.

Lucy likes to lick, especially to groom Daddy's forehead. She's very intense about it, ensuring she doesn't miss a spot. Sometimes she washes his face while he's lying down resting. Other times she starts cleaning when he picks her up to cuddle.

When asked for a "kiss, kiss", she's more likely to oblige Mama with a lick on her nose. When I cup her face in my hands and gently press my lips to the top of her head, Lucy often responds by tilting her head toward my face and giving an affectionate little lick.

Grooming Daddy

Kisses for Mama

Pawsicle

My husband gets the credit for coining the term 'pawsicle' for one of Lucy's habits. Rather than suck on a soother or lick a lollipop, a rear paw is her preference.

Being the dog interpreter of the household, I observe that Lucy turns to this habit to calm herself in times of stress. I've discovered that often it's alleviated by inviting Lucy outdoors. We do let her out at regular intervals, about four hours on average, but sometimes she has additional business to tend to – more urgently.

While Lucy receives a lot of attention, especially when everyone's home, there are inevitably times when we humans have to take care of matters less interesting to dogs, like paying bills. She is patient while her humans are on the phone or laptop, yet after awhile we notice she may out of boredom tend to her pawsicle.

Another reason behind the rear paw licking is simply grooming. Even if I've already rinsed her feet after returning from a walk, Lucy goes over them again. Occasionally she'll find something stuck to her pads, like those sticky tree buds that cover the grass during springtime.

Winter is another matter. The cold, dry climate in South Dakota is harsh on doggy feet. When temperatures plummet well below freezing, we have insulated waterproof booties, secured by fasteners and drawstrings, for Lucy to wear. These are not a fashion statement. Finding a design that she could steadily walk in and that would not fall off en route was a challenge.

Despite best efforts on Lucy's part and ours to prevent her tender tootsies from cracking, we have a natural remedy: pure vitamin E oil. Lucy loves it! Yes, she likes to lick it. So it's best applied while she's snoozing, massaging it thoroughly over and between her toe pads. Once she detects the scent, however, she's off and licking...again.

During warmer weather, when more dogs are out and about the neighborhood, Lucy lets me know when she wants to meet one by a gentle but firm tug on her leash. Before any encounter, I ensure the other dog is friendly. For a girl of 14, Lucy can still pass for a puppy. Many think she still is, especially when she does her frisky little spring dance around a younger male dog her size.

She's a popular gal, our Lucy. When we walk past houses we can hear multiple dogs barking, some peering through windows, tails wagging. Others rush around from back or side lawns to catch a better glimpse and maybe gain our girl's attention.

Lucy's pawsicles carry her well, trotting with a bounce in her steps. She also enjoys visiting human neighbors, guiding me up driveways of those she hopes will come out to greet her. Sure enough, they do.

Rear Leg Support

Tiny Dog Socks

Quadruple Snort

Lucy's a small dog, weighing just over 13 pounds at present. But my, does she have a big snore! Generally, she rests quietly; but every so often...there it is.

Actually, more often she snorts. Four times in a row shows she's content. She may have just finished fluffing up her bed and nestled in a comfortable position. Or she hears her pet parent's voice and acknowledges in like manner. We'll playfully banter back and forth with various verbal sound effects.

Another way Lucy shows she's content is by smacking her lips, as though she's tasting something. Maybe she's reliving her delicious dinner, tummy now full, relaxing as she drifts off to sleep.

What *do* dogs dream about? Some say they relive happy moments with their family. That's a heartwarming possibility. It's amusing to watch Lucy's legs move while she's asleep on her side. Is she chasing bunnies? She occasionally lets out muffled barks, sounding as though coming from a long distance away. Is she communicating with other dogs in her dreams?

Even with us humans, more is related via attitude and non-verbal gestures than words. When Lucy quietly enters a room, she approaches my husband or I with a gentle nose bump on the shin – her way of letting us know she's there.

We are accustomed to her presence when we're moving about the house. Still, to be on the safe side, Lucy wisely finds a secure spot under a table or a chair, or alongside a couch or dresser where she's not at risk of getting stepped on. Out in crowded public spaces, we keep her on a close lead, in our arms, or safe up in her doggy stroller.

Wherever Lucy is in her secure space, that's when you'll most likely hear her do a quadruple snort.

All Four Up

Daddy's Lap

Lucy has lots of favorite spots around the house. Sometimes she curls up in her cozy doggy bed; other times she stretches out diagonally in it. When she wants even more space to herself, she leaps from one couch to another, where she slumps down alongside a corner pillow.

Some cooler places are on the carpet under the desk, against a dresser, or alongside the couch by the door. Even more so, she finds relief from the heat on the cold linoleum kitchen or bathroom floors – leaning up against the wall or tub where she knows she's better protected in the dark.

Once in awhile, Lucy seems to suddenly disappear. We call her name and search our small house. Where can she be? Eventually we've found her nibbling behind the large living room chair, where she may have stashed a treat earlier in the day. Sometimes she's simply licking her pawsicle in peace. For even more privacy, she's discovered the walk-in closet, accessible behind a curtain. Naturally cool inside, it's a quiet place to sit.

A kitchen mat and a bedroom runner rug are her go-to places to savor a treat or bone. Often, though, she'll be so excited to receive one that she stops short once she reaches the living room carpet. There she promptly lowers her rear legs, grasps the reward upright with her two front paws, then begins to gnaw away with her sharp teeth.

Lucy is not just after comfort, relief, privacy, or food. She also seeks out human contact. I enjoy reading on the couch beside her. I reach out to pet her and she wiggles her body closer. Eventually she's shifted adjacent to my thigh, her legs tucked into my leg. As long as she's not held for long periods of time, she accepts being picked up and cuddled.

If I'm the only one home – or awake – she'll sit on Mama's lap. But once Daddy enters the room and sits down, she's eager to jump on the big couch, cross over from his left side and position her upper body on his right leg. There she's most content: on Daddy's lap.

Lucy's Favorite Spot

Chutzpah

Have you ever used or heard this term? She sure has chutzpah to pull off such a feat. It's more than guts. It takes boldness, initiative. Size is no matter, as it's more about attitude, how you carry yourself.

On first meeting Lucy, one would think she's meek and mild. Mostly, she is. She is so patient, not begging for scraps but content with whatever she receives. Rarely does she complain, even if in need. Rather than demand, she waits for a response.

Yes, there are occasions when she speaks up – literally. She's quite capable of jumping up on the couch, as long as she exercises momentum on her approach. But if she's tired, or sees a snack she wants to closer inspect, or she's simply eager to settle onto Daddy's lap as soon as possible, she'll sit by the edge and look at one of us. She progresses to talking in a gentle growl, then a louder bark if needed to get our attention.

Lucy may be little, but she's a big dog on the inside. She has a sense of duty to protect her pet parents and her property. A uniformed mail carrier is perceived as a threat approaching the mail box. So Lucy stands tall along the top of the couch, putting her whole body into loud, successive barks to warn not to come any closer. She really lets a courier have it if they deliver a package to our doorstep. Lucy is convincingly aggressive in her posture and tone.

As a side note, most of the parcel deliveries are for Lucy, so once the courier exits our property, Lucy is eager for us to open the box and see what's inside. She's like a little child, excited to get a present. Her eyes light up; she can't stay still. But she goes further; she sniffs and wags her tail before peering inside the box. Expectantly, she eyes the holder of the crinkly bag, in hopes of sampling some new or familiar treat.

But Lucy guarding her territory is not limited to home. Lucy adapts to changing boundaries. Once we've set up camp somewhere, even for just a night or two, Lucy's protective instinct kicks in. She's already figured out the perimeter of our site, over which no one dares cross. She understands that the tent is our temporary home and she's the first to enter. Her spot is between our shoulders, where she benefits from double body warmth during the cooler early morning hours.

One time at the house I'd exited through the back door and re-entered through the front. That threw Lucy off. I'd barely got the door partly open, when there she was – guarding access to the living room, barking at the would-be intruder. Once she realized it was me, she backed down and enthusiastically welcomed me with a tail wag.

Like my aunt Sylvia recognized, dogs often have more reliable discernment about people than we humans do. When friends arrive, though, she may need a little reassurance that it's okay they enter our house. One time out on an afternoon walk, we were turning a corner on the sidewalk. A tall, grandfatherly figure happened to cross the street and be walking in the same direction. Personally I perceived no threat. Yet Lucy turned around, stopped at the man's ankles, looked straight up at his face, and warned him with a series of bow wows. Don't you touch my mama! The kind-looking man smiled and waited. Assuring Lucy we were not in imminent harm, we continued on our way. Now *that's* chutzpah!

Guarding our Tent

Doggy Cave

You may have heard of a 'man cave', but what about a doggy cave? Like a cat, sometimes a dog just wants her own space, a place to hide out.

Lucy claimed the space under a side coffee table, accessed via a gap between two corner couches. It's just wide enough for her to fit through.

When she first enters, she appears as though she's trying to dig a hole – perhaps to China? Maybe she hopes to connect with her ancestors? The short pile carpet is durable to withstand her front paw exercises. They are probably a healthy workout for her.

Her designated doggy cave is a place to be quiet and untouched; it's where she can de-stress from whatever's bothering her. Soon, though, she comes back out for more attention.

Several years back, at a family gathering at a cousin's place, the women selected me to go spy on the men. Specifically, since I had the big camera, I was to scope out the men's cave, to see what they were actually doing out there. Initially, I peered through windows but then I was more direct. I came through the door to observe what men do when they are not around the women. What I discovered and reported back was not top secret material. The guys were hanging out, beverages in hand, talking around the boat parked in the garage, surrounded by toys – I mean, tools.

Hmm...what would women do in our own cave? Like Lucy, I value a peaceful environment. Some natural ambience is always welcome, just not excessive noise. When you live in tight quarters, sometimes you just have to make do with what you have...to find solitude however you can, whenever you can.

Hidden in Plain View

Kibble Trail

There's a children's story where the wise kids (in pre-GPS days) left themselves a trail of cookie crumbs so that they could find their way back. Lucy's pattern likely doesn't serve the same purpose.

She prefers tiny bite-sized kibble for her little Shih Tzu teeth. They're easier to swallow whole. Though she may eat a small portion of food sometimes by noon, she prefers to eat most of her day's rations between suppertime and bedtime. She seems to like the quiet, having the kitchen all to herself.

As I observe from the living room, Lucy withdraws a piece of kibble, hurriedly trots off with it, deposits it on the living room carpet, then returns to her bowl to repeat this process. But before she stockpiles too much kibble onto the carpet, she goes back to consume the morsels. It's like she made her own built-in calorie reduction, traversing back and forth to retrieve another bit.

For Lucy, food is not a mere necessity – it's entertainment. She often likes to play with her food before eating it. Besides lining up kibble one at a time, then returning to gobble up the trail she's created, she may suddenly pounce on a tidbit without warning. It's as if she's overcoming her prey, displaying her victory. When she's especially energetic, she'll repeatedly toss a piece of kibble around the room. Most times she finds it of her own accord, but other times she enlists someone from her human family to help her find it.

One of Lucy's games is to guess in which hand a treat is concealed. She sniffs both out. Rubbing the scent into both hands may fool her momentarily, but she always gets it right in the end. The stronger scent wins out. She also likes to play 'hide and seek'. We'll tuck a treat or bone into a robe pocket, under a couch cover, or behind a pillow. Ever ready for a challenge, she perseveres until she discovers the hiding spot.

Lucy follows a kosher doggy diet. We don't eat pork or shellfish, so these are not flavors she is accustomed to eating. So when the vet prescribed a heartworm prevention pill, Lucy refused. No additive was sufficient incentive to swallow that nasty-smelling cube. Then we discovered it was supposedly pork flavor. Once we switched to another manufacturer, producing the same medicine, same dosage, but in beef flavor, Lucy loves it. She readily eats it like a treat once a month. Problem solved.

Nibbling Away the Trail

Caught a Squeaky Fish

Treat Toss

Lucy knows that word, whatever form it takes. The word 'treat' evokes excitement. Any movement toward her storage cupboard results in her sudden appearance. Once a door is unlatched, she pokes her head in to sniff and explore. She is especially attuned to the sound of crinkling plastic bags.

We discovered a healthy lamb treat Lucy really liked, but the product was discontinued. Her previous treats contained added soy, which we try to avoid. Now she seems to like her sweet potato chew just as much.

Now, you think of most big dogs gulping down a treat as fast as they can. Not little Lucy. She may decide to toss it first, several times. Once she's had her fun, she settles down on the carpet to enjoy her treat.

Once in awhile, I'll find Lucy swiping her paw at something under the edge of the couch. Sure enough, she had a treat stashed there. It may not be fresh anymore, but that's no matter. It's hers and now she wants it. She eagerly retrieves it from my hand after I extricate the item from some tight spot.

One of her chewable tablets is flavorful enough that she looks forward to taking it. No incentives needed. We simply hand her the pill dosage and she readily eats it in seconds flat. Well, most of the time, that is. When a playful urge comes upon her, she takes delight in tossing the pill over her shoulder, looking for it, then throwing it around some more. We have to keep an eye on where it lands, since it can camouflage into the carpet.

Treats and pills are not the only things that Lucy tosses around. Her favorite games include pulling our socks off, throwing then fetching her fish, and shaking one of her stuffed toys like a rag doll.

Weenie Dog is one of her oldest toys. She interacts with him as though he's a real friend, showing tender compassion. I move him about like a puppet, doing the '*mon cheri*' routine. When Lucy's had enough of his playful nose rubs, then chomp!

With Lambchops Lucy relates differently. She tackles him and uses her snout to punch him in the stomach until he squeaks. But she also has a gentler side, resting her snout on him like a pillow.

The Sock Tug is On

Green Bone

Lucy wants a green bone? That was a question that really caught her attention, over which she went ecstatic. Even if we happened to mention the color green in casual conversation, Lucy would perk up and wait expectantly. One trick I taught her was to gently remove the bone I held out for her between my teeth.

Upon discovery of this dental treat, we were pleased how much Lucy liked it, how well it cleaned her teeth, as even our vet noted. She would receive one daily before bedtime. Though she usually chomped on it right away, occasionally she would hide it somewhere obvious. We'd find it in a corner by the closet or at the edge of a full-length curtain. Pretending to sniff out her hiding place, Lucy would try to throw me off track with a decoy sniff in another direction. She's an adept strategist! For a greater challenge, one time she hid her green bone under camouflage, by a green bag on the floor.

This year we learned from a dog nutritionist that this particular dental treat was way too high in protein for Lucy. Since it contains no meat, we were surprised and disappointed. How hard it was to give her one last bone, then offer the remaining packages to our neighbors' dogs!

Fortunately the nutritionist recommended another dental treat which is substantially lower in protein. The shape's not as appealing; still we ordered these for Lucy, and she likes to chew on these ones for even a longer duration. Hopefully they also give her teeth a more thorough cleaning.

Presenting bones in a playful manner is added incentive to clean her teeth.

Lucy Wants a Green Bone

Fresh Water

Le'at, le'at (Slowly, slowly) Lucy lurks like a lion to her kitchen water dish. The first time I observed her in slow motion like this, I was concerned maybe she was having a stroke. Thankfully, she was not. We don't know what's behind this behavior. Her dishes are beneath an overhang in the counter, bordered by cupboards on both sides. Maybe she's cautiously approaching to be sure no one's going to jump out at her? Once she's satisfied the coast is clear, she begins to lap, lap, lap then swallow her cool fresh water.

It must be fresh. No floaters, no residue. And cool, not setting in sunlight for long. Why settle for less?

Lucy has an alternate water dish, metal rather than glass, beside the tub. That room generally stays cooler, so it's her preferred watering hole. Once while we were visiting friends, we noticed Lucy was missing. Where's Lucy? Then I realized aloud, "Oh...she's gone to the bathroom." My friend looked momentarily alarmed until I clarified. Lucy must have gone in search of the bathroom, expecting there she would likewise find a dish of water! Sure enough, there she was. We rectified the situation and gave her a refreshing drink.

Back at home, Lucy will open the door with her nose or paw if it's slightly ajar. Sometimes she needs guidance to find her way to the water dish, as she becomes disoriented in the dark. So we added an automatic night light. When visibility is clear, she actually hurries to the bathroom dish!

Just like us, sometimes dogs need to be encouraged to drink more water to prevent risk of dehydration when temperatures soar. You know the saying: you can lead a horse to water, but you can't make him drink it? Well, we can bid Lucy to come. She may follow us to her water dish. But then she may sit there and refuse to drink. Stubborn spurts can be a Shih Tzu trait. Patiently I sit with her, stroking her back, urging her in a loving tone to take some sips. She dips her head...and no splashes, no sound. Lucy, you can't fool Mama. Eventually, if only to please me, she stops pretending and actually takes a few slurps. Good girl!

Our neighbor Judy adores our dog. We bring her over for visits. She bought her a birthday gift of a blue travel bottle. It carries about a quart of water. When squeezed, it spurts into the fountain top cup. So Lucy always has fairly fresh water for the road.

My husband also purchased a more portable red rubber dish. It collapses into a flat disk and fits in our glove compartment, ready to pocket and fill on the go for short outings. So Lucy never needs to go without fresh water.

Tub Side Water Bowl

Thirst is Quenched

Breath Test

Occasionally we go to a social event where we cannot bring Lucy. Either dogs are not allowed, or the environment is not conducive to her health and well being. It may be too noisy, such as fireworks or air shows. Or it may be too hot, without sufficient shade or air conditioning. We miss her, and she misses us – even if it is for only a short time.

Upon our return home, she wags her tail with excitement. I pick her up and cuddle her. Then she turns her head, looks me in the face and sniffs my breath! What did I eat while away?

Lucy has several favorite foods which she receives as appetizers to her staple wet and dry dog foods. Saying the word ‘chicken’ really gets her attention; so does the word ‘popcorn’. She positions herself as though leaning on her elbows, paws curved inward, head up, watching any movement toward and around the kitchen. We give her a small morsel of lean chicken breast, or a few puffy pieces of popcorn.

Other foods safe for dogs, and particularly for Lucy in tiny amounts, include: roast beef, turkey breast, grilled salmon or white fish, boiled broccoli, steamed cauliflower, fresh green beans, baked sweet potato, unsweetened natural applesauce, and mashed blueberries (an excellent antioxidant).

As an incentive to go along with her new wet dog food, a dog nutritionist recommended a small portion of pasta. Periodically Lucy looks forward to a few strands of plain spaghetti before eating the cut-up pieces in her main course. On the rare occasion that her tummy is upset, she takes to boiled rice, perhaps with a teaspoon of unsalted chicken broth. During Passover, she readily partakes of little bits of *matzah* with us. A dab of plain yogurt or a smidge of cream cheese once in awhile helps the medicine go down.

While much of a dog's senses are taken up with food smells, out on "poo poo" walks – as my husband calls them – a lot of data gathering occurs en route. I wonder how specific urine odors correspond to different types of dogs? Can Lucy tell whether it was a Saint Bernard or a Chihuahua which left that mark?

Typically, people open the back door for their dogs (or provide their own mini dog door) to let them do their business on their own. Not so with Lucy. She expects us to accompany her – whatever the weather! Then she takes her time to decide on the best spot to squat. Providing we're not in a hurry to be somewhere, that's okay. When my husband takes her out, she often just sits there. She waits for Mama to enter the yard, then pees on demand!

Of course, we let Lucy have time to enjoy her yard, to relax in the green grass, to sniff around the rabbit trails. She knows these animals by name: bunny, dog and kitty cat. Upon mention, she looks around, especially if we make 'meow' sounds. One winter night, Lucy seemed unsettled, going around sniffing along edges of rooms. It turned out she scoped out a mouse in the house! Another time she chased away a whole flock of Canadian geese gathered at the riverside.

But then there was a time she was not so brave. A baby horse was wandering around the grounds of an historic site. The curious creature bent down to investigate our little lion dog. Lucy looked horrified and scampered away. Yet the horse persisted in trying to befriend her. So Lucy kept on the alert. Another time at our friends' hobby farm, a baby goat went to check out our small dog. Lucy became alarmed when said goat stepped up on my back while I was attempting to shield her!

A safer alternative, Lucy found, is the inanimate little *shofar* (ram's horn) setting on a lower shelf of our living room. Every so often, she'll walk up to it and take a whiff.

Smelling that Aroma

Slurping a Noodle

Beddy Bye

Lucy, do you want to go "beddy bye"? Yes, she knows the term and responds to the question. A tail wag is affirmation. Moving into the bedroom, patiently waiting beside the bed for a lift up is further indication of her understanding.

Sometimes she needs a preliminary prompting. We have a rhyming little jingle: "pee pee, before sleepy". Lucy knows a trip to the back yard is in order.

Other times, it's Lucy who drops not-so-subtle hints that it's bedtime. First she stares, then sighs, then stretches out by my feet – all in stages. Next, emphatically, she gets up and heads to the bedroom, sitting beside the bed. If I've not acknowledged her wishes promptly enough, she reminds me with a "grrr" sound emanating from the next room. That's my signal that it's time to shut down the computer and listen to Lucy's wisdom. She's usually right in that regard. When I've stayed up late to work on something, it's often diminishing returns.

Lucy knows she's been heard when she sees me closing windows, locking doors and shutting off lights. She stands and postures herself to rise to the next level. I reach down and gently pick her up, placing her in the middle of the bed.

There, instantly, she flops down onto her side. I bid her goodnight with a pet and a kiss on the top of her head. Sometimes I'll read for a few minutes. By the time the bedside lamp is turned off, or at some point during the night, Lucy softly moves up by my side. She knows she's safe there. My husband and I are part of her pack and she wants to be with us.

Camouflaged on Quilt

Window Seat

When I fly I prefer a window seat. When I'm sitting at a desk, even if mostly looking at a computer screen, I still like to be able to face out a window, to have natural sunlight.

Lucy likes windows too, but she's not tall enough to look out. So what does she do? First, she jumps up on the couch; then she takes a leap up along the back. Carefully she turns around and seats her bottom on the top of the couch back. Her rear legs stick straight out, feet flat against the wall. Her posture reminds me of a toddler. Lucy leans forward, her front legs balancing on the window sill. Elbows are out, paws turned inward.

If one of us is sitting on the couch, she may motion with her eyes to elicit a hand up onto the seat. Without asking, she may go ahead and climb up one of her humans like on a step ladder to reach the top. My husband's shoulders are a broad enough place for her to turn around and make a U-turn, if it suits her to face a different direction.

Lucy takes her role as window watcher seriously. Not only does she bark to ward off any potential encroachment on our property, she also alerts my husband that Mama's arrived home. With a swing of her head, she tells him, "Ruff"! I see her and smile, calling her name as I approach the front of the house. Similarly, I let Lucy know when Daddy is home, and she looks out the window, wagging her tail as he comes closer into view.

Whether basking in some sun rays, or taking in a cool breeze, Lucy can sit like that at the window sill for quite awhile. She looks for kids playing, or for dogs on walks. When she's had enough sightseeing, she may choose to straddle the couch top like a motorbike and recline along the edge, resting with her head turned to one side.

Sometimes I'll nap beside her on the lower level, the main couch seat. Lucy provides a picturesque example of Sabbath rest.

Positioned to Observe

Chasing Bunnies

Rabbits are among the animals who share our yard. Lucy doesn't pay much mind to squirrels, although they may chatter and squawk at her – as if she has no right to be there! One even halted on the overhead power line (aka squirrel highway), waiting for Lucy to move from the ground beneath. Don't they realize dogs can't jump that high?!

We also have an assortment of little birds, which perch more in the front trees, by the feeder and baths set out for them. Quite often we spot a cardinal or two. One day, a couple of Mallard ducks greeted Lucy through the fence of an adjacent yard. She didn't know what to make of these big creatures quacking at her!

Anyhow, back to the bunnies. During springtime we've found places around the property where newborns are tucked for safekeeping. Or so their mother thought. We have to be careful in removing leftover fallen leaves from the fall. The little ones resemble mice, and sure can scream loudly when accidentally picked up by human hands!

Rabbits are really cute once they can fend for themselves. They dart out from among our lilies. I watch as one poses like a statue upon spotting our dog. Lucy simply does her business and feigns not to notice. Suddenly, like lightening, Lucy dashes from her squat and heads straight for the bunny! Usually, though, she takes her time sniffing around the yard, following the bunny trails. Then, once she finds a rabbit, the high-speed chase is on. Bunny circles that way, then abruptly changes direction. Lucy catches on, and follows suit. They're comical to watch, encircling around. Eventually, the bunny makes it to one of its known exit points – either a hole in the fence, under the gate, or the gap beside the shed.

Now I don't think Lucy would actually hurt a rabbit were she ever to catch up to one. She even seemed to show mercy to a bunny on a cold winter's day; she came within less than three feet, but let it get away.

Relaxing on the Alert

Friendly Initiatives

Lucy is quite the sociable little dog, so she has a wide circle of friends, spanning three countries!

Closer to home, we were walking one of her favorite routes, when she began to urge me forward more quickly. Unusually, she pulled on her leash and made tiny whine sounds. She seemed eager to catch up to a couple of people she'd never met before! Curiously I picked up the pace. Once we reached them, we were all surprised as Lucy reveled in their attention.

Another time we were walking in the neighborhood, Lucy spotted a man donning a dark hood. He wasn't even on the same side of the street, but Lucy didn't like him being even that close. She glared at him, loudly growling to dare not come near us.

Some dogs Lucy is keen on meeting, motioning for us to walk the same direction. Other dogs...not so much. Once, my husband and I were browsing in an antique shop, when we encountered a huge spotted dog. Lucy's eyes grew wide in fear and she hid, peering out from behind Daddy's legs.

My husband recounted that before I met them, Lucy had nearly been attacked by a pit bull. Thankfully, she was not hurt. More recently, a large terrier-type dog suddenly bounded from someone's front yard, unleashed, and viciously lunged at Lucy. I yelled, swooped her up to safety in my arms, and the owner rushed out to restrain his dog. Lucy was crying like I'd never heard her before. Upon careful inspection, I found no bite marks. I severely warned the property owner that his dog better not ever be loose like this again, and he profusely apologized.

Lucy's original vet Dr. Dayton, of blessed memory, was an extraordinarily kind man. He showed genuine affection toward animals before beginning any examination or treatment. You could see the care in his eyes. We attended his community memorial.

Finding another vet with such skill and compassion was a challenge. Over time, Lucy's needs have changed. We had a good interim vet clinic. Seeking a second opinion on a matter of Lucy's heart medication, we ended up going with another vet. Likely from birth, Lucy's had a murmur. We want the best for her. Fortunately, we did not remain with this other vet. We credit our current veterinary team with being instrumental in saving Lucy's life. That's a story for another chapter.

At this moment, Lucy is in the capable and caring hands of her long-time groomer, Marilyn, who welcomes her with a smile and open arms. She has a big heart and pays attention to the little details. Shih Tzu dogs are hypoallergenic and do not shed. I hate for Lucy to lose her beautiful golden curls four times a year, but if we didn't take her for a haircut, her fur would just keep on growing. During South Dakota's warm seasons, Lucy would be panting intensely from the heat. So for her sake, we forsake her rich, shiny coat. I've tried grooming Lucy, and have successfully managed touch-ups, but for a real professional stylish look that she deserves, we go to Marilyn. Lucy emerges, tail wagging, her body wiggling and looking half her size!

Most of the time, Lucy comes with us wherever we go. For the few instances where we've had to fly, we're thankful for our trusted dog sitters. Of special note is Rachel, who's cared for Lucy on a number of occasions early on in our marriage. In fact, she watched over our little one leading up to our wedding in Canada, until after our honeymoon in Israel. Jay and Peggy welcomed Lucy into their home while we took a return trip to visit friends in Israel during Passover. Then, Ed and Julie watched over our baby girl at their house for a long weekend during which we flew out for my father-in-law's 80th birthday reunion. As hard as it was to be away from Lucy, knowing she'd miss us for those weeks, we knew she was in trusted hands.

Lucy shares with us an extended family comprised of close friends. Our Israeli friends Malka, Avigail, Hannah and Kati have met Lucy via video chat. They adore her and often ask how she's doing. Lucy has an honorary *bubbie* in New York. Perrie proudly pushed our fur baby around in her stroller as we walked around a few sights together. Uncle Asher shared a bench with Lucy around an outdoor patio table. Aunt Violet and Mama Anna delight in Lucy, hosting us in their homes in Toronto. Big sisters Carol and Tish have provided much prayer backing for Lucy's health. Among the faithful few who keep in touch via snail mail, Heidi and Lewis are always sure to address the envelope and letter to Lucy as well.

Beckoning Eyes

Dog Greetings in Philly

Chomping Through the Snow

Like a child, Lucy loves fresh-fallen snow. Her eyes light up, she pauses at the first snowfall, then she playfully romps in it, scooping up mouthfuls of this refreshing hydration. It's a joy to watch her.

I think back to when I used to take my friend Cheryl's dog Abby out for walks. One time we were going through a school ground, when Abby quickly lunged for something. With fast reflexes, I reached down, grasped her jaw and tilted her head downward, causing the object to drop. It turned out to be a chicken bone! I removed the hazardous object which could have caused her to choke, or splintered inside her.

Abby looked up at me with an expression of betrayal I won't forget. How could you deprive me of something good? The lesson I derived from her chomping on that bone that day was profound. Sometimes we think God seems unfair when He prevents us from getting something we think is good. But He's so much wiser... He knows the bigger picture and foresees the consequences.

Letting Lucy chomp on clean snow poses no harm. She won't stay outside for long if the temperature is too cold. One of her pet parents is always out there with her. When it's excessively freezing, she wears her pink coat which our neighbor Judy purchased for her.

Her booties protect her from frostbite, or prevent painful ice wedging between her toes while out on walks around the block. We've had some deep freezes here in South Dakota. During these days, we shovel a track around our backyard so Lucy has a safe place to exercise in short bursts at a time. We aim for a couple of laps each time she goes out to relieve herself. Without this path we create, Lucy's little legs would get stuck in the deep fallen snow.

New Boot Tryout

Road Trip

Lucy began her life on a road trip. She was born while her doggy parents and their human family were away at the lake. She's familiar with the term "road trip" and becomes excited so long as she's assured she's coming with us.

We avoid packing in her view, especially if one of us is going on a flight where she cannot come. We've noticed how she begins to nervously pace. She likes when we all remain together.

Even on shorter day outings, or weekend camping trips, Lucy shows enthusiastic relief once she sees evidence that she's included in the plans. I make a point of showing her leash, her food and water dishes. She has her own travel pillow and blanket. Once when I pulled the tent out into the living room, I asked if she wanted to go in it and Lucy poked her nose into it.

Kind neighbors looked after Lucy periodically during the first couple of years of our relationship, when William traveled back and forth to visit me in Canada. Looking back, I realize what a sacrifice it was for little Lucy, to be without Daddy during those times.

Due to the size of her snout, considered a breathing liability by some domestic airlines, she was not able to accompany us on all travels. Since South Dakota has no direct international flights, that also ruled out Lucy coming with us to visit and volunteer in Israel. Though she was safe with trusted neighbors, we missed her dearly and checked in with them regularly. Even as I write this chapter outside on our patio, Lucy is seated on my lap, receiving cuddles.

When we go on family road trips, Lucy has various riding positions. She likes to rest her chin on the passenger's inner elbow, facing the driver. Typically, that's when Mama's in the passenger seat. Once she's ready to stretch out, she beckons to move into the back seat, where she has her own cushioned lounge chair cover. That surface keeps cool in the hot sun. Occasionally Lucy watches out the windshield from the center of the back seat.

In preparation for our 2023 road trip to Canada, we ordered a special gift for Lucy's birthday out of my husband's work reward points. It doubles as both a doggy stroller and a car seat. Lucy likes it! At ground level, she can climb in and out on her own when she wants to rest. From the higher vantage point on wheels, she often sits up and looks around at her surroundings. Her "Goldsmobile", as we nicknamed it, gives her more access to coffee shops, restaurants and malls. Inside a vehicle, temperatures can rapidly soar or drop beyond outside conditions. So if Lucy's not welcome to come in with us when we're on a road trip, then we go elsewhere.

Why call it "Goldsmobile"? It's a play on words with our family name, in addition to the color tone of the fabric. It looks like a real baby pram, replete with a foldable cover which protects from sun and light rain. A side mesh provides breathing room. Underneath is a storage pouch, which Lucy discovered also makes a comfortable hammock!

When we showed up at my local congregation in Toronto, we encountered some surprised expressions. Upon seeing the buggy, one woman seemed just about to wish us *mazel tov* (congratulations)...until she spotted Lucy's fur! Little Lucy wasn't the only dog who participated in the annual parade in the Jewish community. Amidst the blue and white flags, she sat up in her stroller, protected from the thousands of feet along the route.

In addition to Toronto a few times, Lucy's also been to Times Square in New York. Friends have welcomed her into their homes. Other big cities she's visited with us include: Philadelphia, Boston, Edmonton and Halifax.

Wilderness excursions in the Canadian Rockies involved camping in Jasper National Park. A huge elk stopped near our tent to munch on some leaves. It loudly bellowed. Noticing the large creature curiously observing our little dog, I quickly lifted her up and away from reach into our vehicle.

During our latest family visit down by the Appalachian Mountains, I was attacked by a rooster, who furiously pecked and clawed at my legs! Who'd have thought the bird comprehended my comment, "Look Lucy, those are chickens. You like to eat them." Lucy remained safely in my arms until I eventually escaped into the trailer. She snuggled on the couch beside William's late friend Don's ma Virginia.

Elsewhere at a family cabin in West Virginia, Sammy the Shepherd gave us all a welcome reception. He trotted over to Lucy and dropped his favorite rubber chicken toy at her feet, as if to say, "Let's be friends."

This trip was the last time Lucy saw William's dad; Pa passed away peacefully in his sleep five days later. He is remembered by many as a kind-hearted man.

Backseat Recliner

Mama's Hometown Toronto

Canadian Rockies Excursion

Age Nine Firsts

During Lucy's ninth year, she had several first-time experiences. That was her mama's influence. She'd lived a rather sheltered life with Daddy.

On long hikes, when she tired of walking or when terrain was unsteady, Lucy would ride in a tummy pouch which was strapped to my shoulders. This same device enabled her to come on short bicycle trail rides with us.

For one of her birthdays we bought her a life jacket. That way she could accompany us in canoe rides. She slept in the middle while her pet parents paddled from the front and back. Lucy seemed less certain about swimming while wearing the life jacket. I held her near the end of a dock, treading water, and we stayed in the tolerable lake a few minutes to cool off.

Lucy experienced broader horizons in 2020, the year she stepped into the ocean – on her own initiative – at the Gulf off the coast of Florida. We had traveled that way to visit with my father-in-law.

The next time Lucy reached the ocean was on the Atlantic side of Canada in 2023. We stopped at the famous Pier 21 in Halifax, where the last voyage of the ship Aquitania brought some of my family from Britain to immigrate after WWII. On my father's side, I'm at least a fourth-generation born Canadian.

While William and I took a ferry cruise around Ellis Island and the Statue of Liberty, Lucy was spared a noisy subway ride and relaxed with our friend in her

New York home. Both Lucy and Daddy are America-born.

Lucy crossed her first national border in 2021. Upon disembarking from our vehicle in Windsor, I sang aloud our anthem, “O Canada.” Meanwhile, Lucy began scoping out scents along our walking path.

Goldsmobile at the Atlantic

First Kayak Ride

Wading into the Gulf

Smooth Operation

Finding a lump is a pet parent's dread. It was small, about the size of a ball bearing, on Lucy's left side. We pointed it out to our vet, who advised keeping an eye on it in case it grew. He re-examined it on subsequent appointments and saw no need to take action.

Not until our original vet prematurely passed away did we find that the lump had increased to the size of a pea. The new vet expressed concern and recommended surgery. The lump and its rubbery casing were successfully removed with no further repercussions.

During the post-op healing process, Lucy needed close tending. Mama took on a nursing role. We camped out on the floor together, with Lucy resting in her doggy bed. We made sure she did not jump nor stretch the affected area.

After the first 24 hours, I changed her dressing. Lucy had about a two-inch round patch, stapled, looking rather raw. When it began to seep, I immediately contacted the clinic. Antiseptic swabs were gently applied, and the prescribed medications were administered. Thankfully, Lucy soon healed up with no infection, the bruising dissipated, and staples were removed. Once her fur grew back over the site, we couldn't tell anymore where the incision had been.

The more visible lasting remnant of the surgery was missing teeth! While under anesthetic, the clinic removed a reportedly infected corner tooth. That was regrettable but understandable. But they also took out four of her tiny front teeth! Rare for her breed, Lucy had a beautifully aligned set of teeth. You could see them when she smiled. Shocked, I asked why. They claimed that they were loose!

Overall, it was a smooth operation.

Darling Baby Girl

Bark Mitzvah

Please don't be offended at my Jewish humor. Recently someone told me she likewise referred to her dog's significant birthday.

To shed some insight rather than fur, *bar* refers to a son, and *mitzvah* means commandment. When a boy reaches the age of 13, he's considered responsible for his actions. He trains for a special public ceremony called a *bar mitzvah.* He comes up front in the congregation and reads his selected portion from a Torah scroll. He may also give a short message of his understanding.

Likewise, in some traditions, girls experience a similar rite of passage at age 12, called a *bat mitzvah.*

In case you're wondering...Lucy is a very intelligent dog, but no – she has not learned to read! Perhaps, though, she recognizes some spelling. Knowing she knows certain words that would get her excited, we sometimes spell them out. Once, Lucy reacted to the letters: c-h-i-c-k-e-n! Hmmm...Mmm...

When Lucy turned 12, I took her picture in her backyard mini pool. I posted it on an e-card and sent it out to friends, commemorating her 'bark mitzvah'. Little dogs age at about five times the amount in human years. So our 14-year-old dog is now a senior.

We treasure the time with Lucy and hope she's with us until 18. That's a ripe old age for a Shih Tzu. *Lechaim!* (To life!)

On past birthdays, we've celebrated with Lucy over a barbecue, or over an egg or turkey cake. We've bought her special dog treats or bones. Among prior gifts she's received from us are: stuffed toys, a stroller, a harness, a carrier pouch, a life jacket, winter boots, T-shirts, a winter coat and a travel bottle (from our neighbor Judy), a dish tray, a treat container, travel bowls, a dog bed and blankets (including a special purple one from Aunt Sylvia).

Mazel Tov with a Splash

Miracle Recovery

The second half of Lucy's 13th year, early 2025, she had a close call.

After she vomited yellow bile several times one night, we brought her in to the vet. We left with medications. By week's end, Lucy began to whimper in pain. This vet refused to make time to see her!

With Lucy in the vehicle, I pulled off into a parking lot and began calling neighbors, looking for reliable referrals. Then I went online with my phone and was able to book an appointment that day with our new vet, Dr. Ben.

He thoroughly examined our dog, diagnosed her with a liver condition, and ordered taking her off the medications prescribed by the former vet. One was actually harmful to her, another was ineffective, and the third was an incorrect dosage!

To give her a better fighting chance, we agreed for our new pet hospital team to give Lucy IV treatment over the weekend. By Monday, they said she was barking to come home.

Her treatment protocol continued with a cocktail of at-home prescription medications administered by Mama, her makeshift nurse. At regular intervals, we brought her back to Dr. Ben to check on her progress. Amazingly, her liver levels were steadily dropping. From 10 times higher, and one off the charts, eventually Lucy's core liver value returned to normal, according to the blood work! The infection and swelling was gone! The "sludge" backed up in her gallbladder was effectively cleared as well. We so appreciate our veterinary team for their integral role in saving Lucy's life. We also heartily thank our many friends and family across three countries for praying for Lucy's recovery. Even her hearing has improved!

However, the story does not stop here. The myriad of meds needed to restore Lucy's liver put a strain on her kidneys. A year earlier, the former vet told us that Lucy had renal disease. She was prescribed a special dog food. A year later, her blood work indicated her kidney function was normal. Now her numbers were elevated again.

We were disheartened. But our trusted new vet persevered with a plan. He taught us how to administer a fluid solution under our dog's skin. We hoped that extra hydration, along with resuming an aggressive renal diet, would kick-start her kidneys back into normal range. A natural dog food company has a dog nutritionist on board who offered us a free consultation. Working in conjunction with our vet, feeding Lucy a combination of crushed dry and wet dehydrated food (specially formulated to be low protein, low phosphorus, and low salt), we were all relieved to find that Lucy's next blood tests showed normal kidney function!

Then Lucy had another seizure. The first time I witnessed her having one in 2021 was especially alarming. At first I thought she was having a heart attack. It was localized around her jaw, causing teeth clenching and panic breathing. In all, she's had about 12 seizures now over four years. The last five were different; they were grand mal – full-body shaking. Before, Lucy would pace, sensing one coming on.

Later, the preliminary sign was a curled lip. This past May, my husband called to tell me Lucy was having the worst seizure he's seen. I headed straight home.

For hours afterward, there can be some residual confusion or unsteadiness. Lucy was essentially out of the seizure by the time I was home. With assurance, calling her name, she stood up and wagged her tail. Late that night I let Lucy outside to relieve herself. Suddenly she collapsed and was lying unconscious on the ground! I scooped her into my arms and rushed inside to wake my husband. Though Lucy came to within seconds, we headed straight to the nearest pet hospital. It turned out she'd fainted from lack of oxygen to her brain. Twice more it happened into the next day.

A colleague of our vet fit Lucy in for heart tests. To our knowledge, she's had a heart murmur since birth. Our original vet had prescribed her medication. Now Lucy's on an increased dosage, as well as another type of heart medication. Together, they relieve her heart of having to work too hard and prevent further damage.

Yet the extra medication again put strain on her kidneys, so we've had to continue twice-weekly treatments to help flush them out. Lucy remained steadfast as Mama prepared to apologetically insert a needle horizontally beneath her skin. Initially the built-up fluid gave her a camel hump which soon dissipated. We recall the vast difference this treatment made when first administered by our vet and tech assistant. Within a couple of hours after returning home, Lucy was back to her usual self! She was energetic, eager afresh to eat and drink.

Lucy has a new renal treat she receives after her morning liquid syringe of crushed meds. She readily chews her flavored supper dose. By bedtime she looks forward to a long chew on her low-protein dental bone. With our vet's consent, Lucy is allowed a limited-size morsel of lean meat, mostly on Shabbat or other special holidays.

We give our utmost gratitude to God for His mercy in restoring our furry family member.

Prepared for Medicine

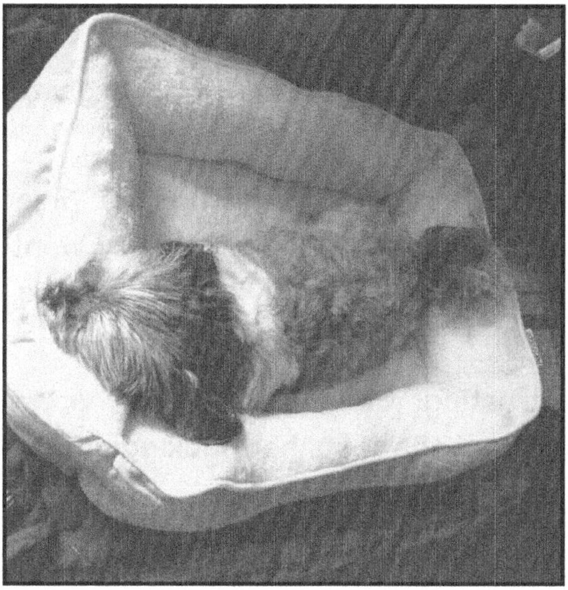

Snoozing in Birthday Bed

Perky and Playful

Welcome Home

Our precious little Lucy is quick to forgive, showing unconditional love.

This week, shortly after giving her injection of hydration to cleanse her kidneys, Lucy wanted to sit on my lap and even licked my right hand, the one that stuck her with a needle.

She's so trusting. Coming back from a walk, after rinsing her feet, she rests her back against my tummy as I dry her tender tootsies.

Lucy loves to be with us, wherever we are. Yet she's always happy to hear the word "home". We give her assurance en route until our actual arrival in the driveway. Then once her feet are planted in the doorway, she wags her tail with joy.

Another of the gifts I picked out for her is a small, heart-shaped pillow, embroidered with the words: "You make my tail wag." Between the yard and back door is Lucy's mat: "Home is where your dog is."

So it's mutual. Welcome home Lucy. We love you, Lucy.

In Mama's Arms

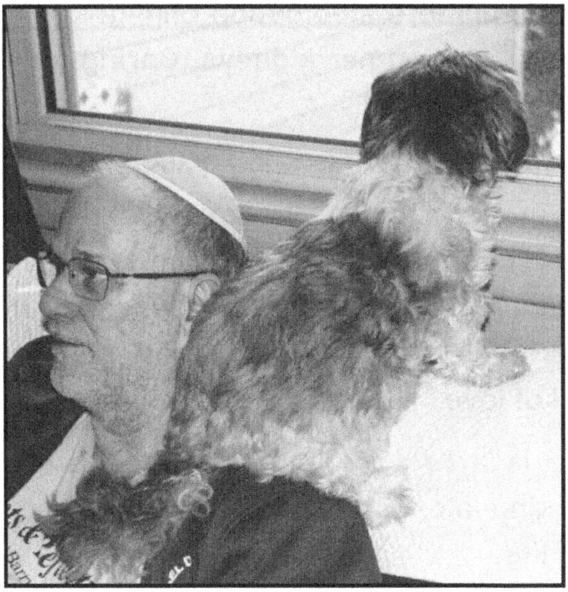

On Daddy's Shoulder

Postscript

December 2025

As I apply polishing touches to this manuscript in preparation for publication, a brief update is in order.

The first of this month, we received news that one of our cherished Israeli friends, Malka (z"l) of blessed memory, is now buried in the Land of Israel she loved.

During Chanukah, our little lion dog exhibited some concerning symptoms. Fainting episodes had returned and increased. This day she was coughing and breathing rapidly. A consequent vet visit led to the cardio specialist making time for Lucy that day. The results explained what we didn't want to hear. Her enlarged heart is showing more signs of strain. So that means more medication changes. What helps her heart is hard on her kidneys. Caring for both is a delicate balancing act.

Marking the end of this year, blood tests showed Lucy's liver and kidney functions to be back in mid-range. She continues on supportive supplements. No more does she receive fluid injections. Her heart has responded well to the new dosages. Lucy has a big heart, full of love.

Our Lucy is a brave girl, and we're determined to keep fighting alongside her for a long and thriving quality of life.

Lucy's Loving Embrace

Gazing Heavenward

References

The American Kennel Club, Inc. 2025 www.akc.org "Shih Tzu History: From Royal Dogs to Beloved Companions"

Foreign languages: occasional Hebrew or Yiddish word transliterations are included in italics.

Note from Lucy

Thank you for buying my book.

May it leave an imprint on your heart.

Author's First Book

www.westbowpress.com

Made in the USA
Coppell, TX
11 June 2026

80835147R00056